WHY ARE MY GOALS NOT WORKING?

Color Personalities for
Network Marketing Success

KEITH & TOM "BIG AL" SCHREITER

Why Are My Goals Not Working?
© 2017 by Keith & Tom "Big Al" Schreiter

Published by Fortune Network Publishing

PO Box 890084
Houston, TX 77289 USA

Telephone: +1 (281) 280-9800

ISBN-10: 1-892366-99-1
ISBN-13: 978-1-892366-99-3

CONTENTS

PREFACE

Before you set your next goal, you have to read this book.

Why?

Because you want to set goals that work for you and achieve exactly what you want. You don't want to achieve someone else's goals. You have one life, and your goals should design the life you want.

Yes, design your own goals. If not, you will end up being a part of someone else's goals. Definitely not fulfilling or fun.

The payoff for designing your own personal goals?

Instead of struggling for motivation, you will be thrilled with every moment that you can work on your goals. When your goals match your personality and values, magic happens.

So yes, goals can work. They do already.

Every day you literally set hundreds or even thousands of little goals, and you achieve them. It is so easy that you hardly give it any thought.

Don't let anyone tell you that goal-setting and goal-achieving are difficult. These activities are not difficult, and you are already a professional.

Want more proof?

How often have you set a goal to go to bed early?

Have you ever set a goal to wake up at a certain time?

Did you set a goal to eat lunch today?

Did you set a goal to watch your favorite television show last night?

You set and achieve these types of goals every day. You are a goal-achievement machine.

Did you ever set a goal to get some ice cream? Maybe you checked your home freezer and found it to be ice-cream-free. So, you put on your coat, climbed into your car, fought traffic, braved the rain, drove to the nearest grocery store, and finally, purchased some delicious ice cream.

There is no stopping us when we are on a journey of goal-achievement.

Now, let's discover how to make our goals work for our network marketing business. We will discover the true foundations of what makes goals work. Then, we can use this discovery to make goal-setting and goal-achieving easy.

Read on and enjoy the exciting future of goals that work for you.

—Keith and Tom "Big Al" Schreiter

A note from Tom:

Because Keith and I co-authored this book, it may be confusing who is writing within a chapter. Any references to heavy metal bands, running, and exercising is Keith. Any references to overeating and conserving energy, that would be me writing at that moment.

BIG AL WORKSHOPS

I travel the world 240+ days each year.
Let me know if you want me to stop in your
area and conduct a live Big Al training.

→ **BigAlSeminars.com** ←

FREE Big Al Training Audios
Magic Words for Prospecting

plus Free eBook and the Big Al Report!

→ **BigAlBooks.com/free** ←

WHERE IT ALL GOES WRONG.

I wanted success. But as a 17-year-old, I wasn't sure what success would mean to me. So I quietly sat in the goal-setting workshop, listening and taking notes.

Business people with thousand-dollar suits, caffeinated salesmen, middle-aged bankers and high-powered executives surrounded me. It wasn't hard to find me in that crowd.

Who was I?

A 17-year-old, long-haired high school student who loved to play drums for a heavy metal band. I didn't fit into this workshop group. But the back of my mind told me, "You want to be successful, so here is your chance to learn how."

The seminar leader was full of himself. He bragged about his cars, his houses, his suits, his travels, and how he was the fastest builder ever in the history of network marketing. Yes, he was a legend in his own mind. And, he was his #1 fan.

I think he drank too many energy drinks that morning. He went from high-intensity to highly-annoying, and it wasn't even lunchtime yet. I felt a little queasy in my stomach.

I struggled. I couldn't relate. In the seminar leader's mind, the only goals worth setting were goals that he wanted in his life. He said things such as, "Don't settle for less. You have to be number one in life. If you are number two, you are just standing in front of the other losers."

I thought, "Well, a new car would be nice. But what am I going to do with a thousand-dollar three-piece suit as a drummer in a heavy metal band? And travel? I still have to go to school every day. I don't care about being number one or crushing the competition. I want to live **my** life, not his life."

Later that afternoon, I succumbed to the pressure of the group. I set my goals. I conformed to the instructions Mr. Intensity gave us. How to be number one in business. How to be number one in sales. How to be number one in relationships. How to be number one in … everything.

Why did I set these goals? Well, as a 17-year-old, I realized everyone there knew a lot more about goals than I did. I just took their advice.

I did what I was told.

I shared my goals with the group. I used other people's goals to inspire me to elevate my goals. I rewrote my goals to be more explicit.

I described each goal in great detail. If it was a car, I wrote down the color, make, model, and every accessory that my car would have. I test-drove and took pictures of me sitting in my dream car. Next, I carefully placed the photos on every mirror of the house. I would see my dream car at every waking moment.

Laser focus?

Yes.

And guess what happened?

Nothing.

I couldn't connect with my goals. I felt no passion for what I had written down. When I woke up in the morning, I didn't feel that motivation to go out and achieve my goals.

But it got worse. Many of my new goals required skills that I didn't have yet. That was cruel.

Cruel? Yes.

Here is what I mean by cruel. Encouraging people to set goals that they cannot reach is cruel. There is nothing more frustrating than knowing what you want, but not having the ability to get there. No amount of chanting and believing will change the fact that if we don't have the skills, we can't get to where we want to go.

So I had goals. But they weren't **my** goals.

Setting goals is easy. Anyone can write down a list of goals. But, setting the right goals is what we want to do. I didn't know that. If we don't have an emotional attachment to our goals, then how can we feel excitement in our pursuit of these goals?

This is why people set goals and then fail to take action.

I just became one of those people.

But I wanted success!

The normal goal-setting approach didn't work for me. That didn't mean I had no goals. It only meant that I did not have the right goals for me. At this time in my life, I was not sure what kind of goals I should have. Lost? Yes, I was lost.

On the plus side, at least the goal-setting workshop introduced me to goal-setting. This was something they didn't teach me in high school.

Now it was up to me to take the next step and create personal goals that were right for me.

FEEL THE FAILURE.

Goals should be a joy to accomplish. When we align our goals with our personalities and values, we feel energetic and happy every day.

Unfortunately, that doesn't always happen. We rush into goal-setting, influenced by others and their agendas. Then, we end up creating goals that aren't right for us.

We instinctively know when our goals aren't right for us. We experience dread, fear, and a lack of passion. We force ourselves to move forward. Want an example of that feeling?

New Year's diet disasters.

Imagine we want to lose weight. Where did we get the weight? Unhealthy eating choices, too much food, and no exercise.

But next year will be different. Why?

Because on December 31, we will set our New Year's goal to lose weight. Setting New Year's goals is a ritual. Everyone does it. Therefore, we should do it too.

We say to ourselves:

"This year is going to be my year."

"This year is going to be different than last year's failure."

"I am 100% committed to my resolution."

"No small goals for me."

"I will clear the pantry and refrigerator of all my junk food."

"I will go shopping for fresh, organic food."

"I will join the local gym and buy a multi-year membership."

"This time, no basic membership at the gym. I will go with the platinum option that gives me access to the gym 24 hours a day."

"New workout clothes are mandatory. Tomorrow I will shop for designer workout clothes. Matching colors will motivate me."

"Let me type my affirmations and paste them on my bathroom mirror."

"I will announce to my friends on social media that this is my year to lose weight."

What happens on New Year's Day?

We are at the gym in our new clothes, ready to get busy. The adrenaline is pumping. We have an incredible workout. We can't wait for tomorrow.

We wake up, eat our healthy breakfast, and again eagerly go to our local gym. The adrenaline is pumping. We have an incredible workout. We vibrate with energy! We can't wait for tomorrow. Yes, we are proud of ourselves.

The next day? A different story.

Our body hurts just thinking about leaving our bed. We can't reach down to tie our shoes. There is no way our arms can control the steering wheel to drive to our local gym. Lying in bed, we order a supreme pizza for home delivery to soothe our depression.

Okay, one bad day. We can live with that. But the next day?

Our arms are still sore. How can they feel numb and hurt at the same time? We remember the great taste of that large supreme pizza. Now we are hungry. But, we have to go to work. Maybe we can buy a few donuts on the way to work. No time for gym torture today.

Where did it all go wrong?

It turns out that we don't like exercise. It sounds good in our minds, but the reality is we find no joy in inflicting additional pain on our bodies.

For someone who enjoys working out, loves socializing at the gym, and experiences mad rushes of adrenaline while pumping iron … then exercising at the local gym make sense. For that person, his or her goals are in alignment with who they are.

Unfortunately, we are not that person.

Sometime our goals are too far outside of our comfort zone. Sometimes we get distracted. But usually our goals fail because they are not in alignment with who we are or who we want to be.

What could we have done differently?

If we look inside, maybe we are a person who values being with our family. In that case, we should choose a different exercise routine. We could play with the children in the swimming pool, rollerskate with the family, or dance with our spouse.

Now we are choosing something that is fun for us, instead of something we dread. Our chances of reaching our goals increase.

What kind of activity should we choose for our goals?

How about an activity that we look forward to?

How about an activity that we will miss on the days we don't do it?

We should choose something fun and enjoyable. Then, we will enjoy every day as we move toward our successful goals.

When we get the right goals.

Can we remember a time when we looked forward to something exciting? Maybe it was when we were children. How did we feel when we woke up on Saturday mornings? Happy? Energized? Two full days of fun with no school? This was the best time in our lives.

We did not have to force ourselves to wake up. We were not grumpy, tired, or unenthused. We couldn't wait to get dressed and go play with our friends. Weekends were awesome. We lived for weekends! All week long we thought about our upcoming weekend.

Motivation and fun are automatic when our goals match who we are as a person.

We don't have to chant affirmations, cut out pictures for our vision board, or meditate in silence visualizing our goals. When we know exactly what we want, every step along the way is fun and fulfilling. We are moving forward to our goals.

How do we know when our network marketing goals are right for us?

Easy. Just look at our actions.

What do most people do on Saturday morning? They want to sleep in and relax after a hard, stressful week at work.

What do happy network marketers do on Saturday morning? We check our back office to look at our sales volume. We check to see if anyone joined our team overnight. This is not a chore; this is entertainment. This is what we want to do.

When our goals are in alignment with who we are and what we want, there is never a problem with motivation. Everything is fun. Everything we do is moving us toward our goal.

Want another example?

Health products. Really?

In high school, I hated homework. Reading books seemed like a waste of time. I wanted to play the drums or be with my friends. And guess what kind of books we had to read in high school? Yes, boring books.

But when I first started in network marketing, I sold health products. My attitude changed. Reading books about health and nutrition became interesting. It was fun to learn new and exciting facts about health. I looked forward to reading about health and nutrition every day.

If there was a lecture about health, I was happy to go. If there was an article on the Internet about nutrition, I eagerly read it.

My goal was to learn everything possible about the products in my business. I wanted to be successful, and product education felt like an important step for me to master.

Want another example of when our aligned goals feel right? When we have natural motivation to achieve our goals?

The dream family holiday.

Saving money is not much fun. But what if we had a goal that was in alignment with our values?

Imagine for a moment that our values include spending time with our family. A goal of a dream family holiday would be exciting. Just thinking about all the memories that it would create motivates us to plan and to execute our plan.

Instead of eating at a fancy restaurant, we would feel good about eating at home to save money for the holiday. Even saving a few dollars here and there would create a feeling of happiness. The entire family would enjoy dropping a few saved coins into our piggy bank.

Would we be motivated? Of course. We would look for every possible chance to save money for our dream family holiday. We wouldn't feel deprived that we missed out on a pleasant experience. Every coin, every dollar that we saved would give us the thrilling feeling that we are closer to our goal.

Want a cool secret about setting the right goal?

Happiness is not only reaching the destination, but happiness also occurs on the journey to our goal.

Consistency.

As we saw in the last chapter, when we have the right goal, we experience happiness while achieving that goal. The path to the goal is not distasteful, painful, or boring.

We want to ask ourselves, "Will we enjoy the journey to our new goal?"

If the journey is enjoyable, then consistency is easy. Motivation naturally happens. If the journey is unpleasant, then no matter how big the reward, motivation will be a struggle.

If we are not consistent at our day job, what happens? We get fired.

For example, imagine we wake up on Monday morning and decide not to go to work. We don't call, we don't email, we just don't show up. Will we get fired right away? Maybe, maybe not.

On Tuesday morning, we wake up and decide not to go to work. We don't let anyone know that we will not show up. Will we get fired? Maybe, maybe not. Maybe our boss leaves a voicemail message for us. Well, we ignore it.

If we do this for an entire week, what will happen? There is a good chance that we will be fired. Our boss does not want to pay us for not showing up.

It is the same in network marketing. If we avoid productive activity for a day, we won't be fired. If we avoid productive activity for several days, what are we doing? We are firing ourselves. We are not going to get paid.

Consistency? Very important.

Consistency can work for us, or against us.

Against us? Of course. Here is an example.

It stinks.

Imagine that we have a clever idea to not take a shower today. Acceptable? For a day, sure. A little extra deodorant or perfume and we are good to go.

Tomorrow comes, and we continue our shower embargo. Hmmm, something doesn't smell right.

Day three? Again, no shower. Some friends may politely remind us to bathe.

Let's face it. After one week, we will stink.

And this is what can happen to our network marketing business. If we avoid productive activity day after day, our business will stink.

We can be consistently good, or consistently bad.

Our choice.

PEOPLE ARE DIFFERENT.

Look around you. People are different. In fact, nobody is identical to you or me.

We have different internal wiring and programs. We have different hair color, hair type, eye color, height, gender, etc. Yes, we are all 100% unique. Even identical twins aren't exactly alike. Sometimes you can't tell the difference, but inside, there are two different people.

We have different experiences. We think differently. We want different things.

One size does not fit all.

That means your goals and my goals will be different. That is okay.

Of course, everyone wants the basics. Food, shelter, love of others, etc. But past the basics, we want different things in our lives. Some examples?

How many restaurants are in our local area? When we are hungry, how do we choose which restaurant to visit? Do we look for the most inexpensive restaurant to save money so that we can spend money in other areas of our lives? Or will we go for the fun experience of trying something new? Do we choose a restaurant so we can be seen at that restaurant by others? Or do we pick the restaurant that has the best-looking food so we can take a selfie with our order? Maybe we want the healthiest meal? Or the biggest meal?

So many choices. So many different goals. And this is only for a very basic need: food. Why so many options? Because each of us has different programs and views of the world. We see and appreciate our world in unique ways.

It gets more complicated. Think about our environment. Did our parents influence our decisions? Do we follow our parents' choices? Or do we have an internal teenage program to be the exact opposite of our parents?

Okay. This is obvious. Different people want different things.

So let's take a look at the different reactions from a goal-setting seminar.

The super-achiever speaker.

Four distributors, with four different personalities, decide to go to a one-day goal-setting workshop.

The guest speaker is the #1 producer with an international organization of tens of thousands of people. He is confident, successful, and looks like he graduated from modeling school.

Hour #1: The speaker begins with, "I am qualified to speak, because I am successful." Sounds great. We wouldn't want to listen to someone unsuccessful.

Hour #2: The speaker says, "Let me show you pictures of my accomplishments." The pictures hold our attention. Slide after slide of:

- New luxury cars.

- Vacation homes.

- Traveling the world.

- Premium seats for sporting events.

- Riding in private jets.

- Drinking $1,000-bottles of wine.

- Eating at restaurants where the food is so fancy, you don't know what you're eating.

- Hiring a private shopper.

Now everyone is dreaming about what could be possible.

Hour #3: The speaker says, "Here are some luxury magazines. Pick out what you want when you reach the next pin level in our business."

Lunch break conversations.

During lunch, the four distributors sit at the same table. Their conversation?

Ron is pumped. "This goal-setting workshop is fantastic. It is like the speaker and I are blood brothers. We think the same. I want to take pictures in front of my new mansion and send them to everybody that was mean to me in high school. Why would someone only have two luxury cars when you can have seven? I can't believe he didn't have a big enough wine cellar. In my future collection, I will have at least 2,000 bottles of ridiculously-priced wine. I will be ready for any dinner occasion. Private shopper? I will have private everything. A private butler, a private cook, a private housekeeper, a private shoe-shiner, and I'm just getting started. Yeah, that speaker may be #1 in the company now, but look out. I will make him #2 before long."

Betsy feels confused. She wonders, "Why doesn't his infinity pool have a waterslide? What is the point of the pool without a waterslide or a diving board? How can you have fun in a boring pool? What's up with his private jet? It only has eight seats. That doesn't sound like a big party. Plus the low ceilings make it impossible for you to dance on the plane. Why would you only eat at stuffy restaurants with tasting menus? Wouldn't it be more exciting to have a big backyard barbecue buffet, or a make-your-own-pizza party? Wine? I don't like wine. But sitting with friends at the local craft brewery and playing games? That would be awesome."

Gary is the quiet one at the table. He only makes one comment. "Only a fool would spend money on luxury items which are taxable. Doesn't the speaker know there are tax-saving benefits with certain low-risk bond investments? We can't get ahead financially by investing in depreciating assets."

Yvette is polite. She waits until everyone at the table finishes speaking before sharing her thoughts. "I am so happy for the speaker's success. He loves his life. When he mentioned a big house, I felt he was speaking to me. If I had a bigger house, my grandkids could stay over and play together. But why the big garage? I only need an extended minivan so I can pick up the grandkids and take them to their activities. How did he get his car so clean? My car is filled with fast food bags and games for my grandkids. I am not sure about traveling the world unless my entire family can come. Instead, I think we could rent a giant RV so everybody will be entertained while we drive to Disney World."

Four distributors. Four different views.

If we joined these four distributors at lunch, which view would feel the most natural to us?

There is no right or wrong point of view.

But analyzing our point of view, and choosing goals to match, is the challenge. How do we know what will work for us?

That gets a lot easier when we learn and combine the two big factors that determine which goals are right for us.

Ready to get started?

THE TWO FACTORS TO MAKE OUR GOALS FEEL RIGHT.

What happens when our goals don't feel right? For some, it is a queasy feeling in the pits of their stomachs. For others, they feel no motivation to start working toward those goals. And for others still, any little fear will stop them from action because they don't feel an attachment to their goals.

Yes, if our goals don't feel right, it might be a waste of time.

But what happens when our goals feel right?

1. We stay excited.

2. We can't wait to start the day.

3. We never procrastinate. This is too much fun.

4. We have no fear. Our goals are larger than our fears.

So let's see how we can set the right goals for ourselves.

Personality + values = our goals.

Here are the two factors that we can use to customize our goals.

1. Our color personality.

2. Our personal values.

Combining these two factors and setting the right personal goals creates magic. Our goal-setting quickly becomes … goal-achieving!

First, we will take a look at our own internal wiring. Almost from birth, we develop a certain view of the world. People call this our personality.

From birth? Let's look at an example.

A family has quadruplets. Within a few months of birth, the parents notice the distinct personalities of each baby.

- One baby loves to explore.
- Another baby wants to cuddle.
- The third baby loves entertainment.
- And the fourth baby desires independence and tries to do everything herself.

The children will carry these personality differences into adulthood.

In the next chapter, we will begin describing the four different "color" personalities. Each personality will have different goals that stem from their view of the world.

Then, we will look at values. We all have values, but we place importance on some values more than others. Again, this will affect our choices for our goals.

Let's take a look at the first personality color, and the goals that would match it.

THE YELLOW PERSONALITY.

This is the first of the four color personalities. If the following description feels right, we are a yellow personality. And if it doesn't feel right, that would only mean that we are one of the other three personalities.

Yellow personalities are people who want to help others. If you want a shortcut, simply remember the word, "help." Yellow personalities find happiness in helping other people succeed and enjoy their lives. Usually they think more about other people than they do about themselves.

Everyone loves yellow personalities. They are the most likable and understanding of all the personalities. Because of their view of the world, we will find many yellow personalities in professions such as:

- Social work.
- Teaching.
- Nursing.
- Massage therapy.
- Ministry.

Can we think of people who are helpful in our lives? They might be yellow personalities. For example, when someone is sick, who is the first to volunteer to help? Or, who worries at every party, wanting to make sure every guest knows they are welcomed?

Do we need more help visualizing a yellow personality?

Think about the princesses in the Disney movies. Cinderella is the perfect example of a yellow personality.

But what about goals for yellow personalities?

Let's imagine a yellow personality. What would that yellow personality want in his or her life to feel happiness and fulfillment? Here are some examples:

- Spending time with the grandchildren.
- A chance to go on a mission trip.
- Remodeling the kitchen to make it more family-friendly.
- A swimming pool in the backyard for the children.
- Organizing a volunteer community group to clean the local parks.
- Funding to research a vaccine to stop a disease.

These goals are in alignment with what a yellow personality might want.

What goals would not be in alignment?

Could you imagine a yellow personality wanting this?

- To earn more money than the next-door neighbor.
- To have a fancier car than his or her sister.

- To amass a huge investment portfolio.
- To train for hours to win the local 10K race.
- To get trophies and plaques of recognition.

No, these goals would not bring happiness to a typical yellow personality. Remember, yellow personalities want to help others achieve these types of goals.

Goal-setting for yellow personalities.

Throughout this book, we will use one common goal example. Our goal? To meet new people for our network marketing business.

It will be easy to illustrate the different personalities with this one common goal.

We will show how the different personalities choose different activities and mini-goals to meet new people for their network marketing business.

Let's start by talking about Belinda, a yellow personality.

Belinda's story.

Belinda loves helping people. Her life revolves around her grandkids and spending quality time with them. She also loves:

- Her company, because their products help people enjoy better health.
- Her commission check, because she can help her grandkids and local charities.

- How her team leaders get bonus checks so they can quit their second jobs, have better family vacations, and more.

What business-building activity fits Belinda's personality?

Every day she wakes up and asks herself, "Who can I help?"

There is no rejection when offering to help people. Rejection comes from having an agenda and attempting to create conditional friendships. The fear of meeting new people goes away for Belinda because of her strong desire to contribute.

People can read our intentions. Maybe it is body language, or the words we use. Belinda finds satisfaction and happiness when she contributes to the betterment of other people's lives. That is why people react to her positively.

So how does Belinda create relationships with almost everyone she meets?

By finding ways to assist her local nonprofit organizations, by helping with fundraising, volunteering at clubs, and participating with local youth groups in her area. All of these groups need volunteers. They welcome Belinda with open arms.

Every day is a "fun" day. Belinda gets to do what she loves to do. She reaches her goals of meeting new people and creating relationships with activities within her comfort zone. For Belinda, every day is a perfect day. What could be better?

Here is an example of how Belinda helps her new contacts. First, she helps them to commit to better health in their lives. She enrolls them in a monthly automatic shipment of health products. Part of the profits from that automatic monthly shipment goes to supporting local charity organizations. This is a win-win-win proposition that makes everyone happy.

Charlie's story.

If there is a volunteer activity that needs help, Charlie is on it. When his neighborhood needed another member on the Board of Directors, he knew he could do it. Community is important for yellow personalities. So what did Charlie do to increase his involvement in his community? Here is a partial list.

- He made the neighborhood more kid-friendly. He organized upgrades for the neighborhood playground.
- He planned the local summer parade.
- He organized more volunteer lifeguards to extend the hours at the neighborhood swimming pool.
- He increased the membership of the community volunteer group.
- He started Friday "drive-in" movie nights at the swimming pool, complete with multi-flavored ice cream treats.

Did Charlie have to ask people to join his business? No. Everyone appreciated his efforts, and of course, wanted to know more about what Charlie did for a living.

Many people joined Charlie's business, but what was even better? They sent Charlie referrals of people they knew who would be great for his business.

Setting goals to meet new people is easy for yellow personalities. But, what about other goals that yellow personalities desire?

MORE GOALS FOR YELLOW PERSONALITIES.

Meeting new people is great, but what else can yellow personalities achieve? Let's take a look at some of their other goals.

The Mom-Mobile.

As a single mom, Linda balances a full-time job and being an attentive parent. When Linda joined network marketing, her first goal was to have one hundred dollars extra every week as a safety net. Then that goal grew to become weekend vacations with the kids. Later, the goal grew to long family holidays.

After going full-time in her business, she decided to go for an even bigger goal. Along came the idea of having the coolest minivan ever for her family. And what kind of options would her minivan have?

- Not a regular DVD player for the back seats, but on-demand satellite TV and movies for every seat.

- Heating and cooling with individual controls for every seat.

- Bluetooth headsets instead of wiring.

- Tray tables for food, games, and homework on-the-go.

- Satellite radio and a karaoke machine.

- A built in mini-vacuum cleaner.

- A hidden trash container and recycling bin.

- And a racing stripe down the side of the minivan to make the children feel sporty.

Linda and the family loved commuting not only to school, but traveling anywhere. She also became the best field trip chaperone ever! Everyone loved riding in the deluxe minivan to field trips, museums, and parks.

Mary's story.

Mary cannot live without her fancy coffees. "Addicted" would be a good word to describe her. Three times a day she travels to local coffee shops to get her caffeine and sugar fix.

Mary used to visit the drive-through coffee shop on her way to work. Now, as a full-time networker, she breaks up her day to visit her favorite coffee shops to meet prospects and her team. Free Wi-Fi and plenty of fancy coffee makes the meetings fun.

What used to be an expensive habit now becomes a business expense. She uses the coffee shop to meet prospects and to train her team.

But Mary's coffee addiction drives her to do more.

Mary turns her empty breakfast nook into an in-home coffee shop. It's a dream come true. She doesn't buy a coffee maker. Instead, she buys a restaurant-quality espresso machine.

She finds a deeper love for her favorite beverage and purchases a designer barista uniform, just for fun.

Now instead of meeting prospects at the local coffee shop, Mary invites them to her own personal coffee shop in her breakfast nook. She also holds meetings with her group at her home. No more meeting room costs and no more overpriced beverages. The group uses their savings to buy extra samples to build their business.

Andy's story.

After losing his brother to depression, Andy wanted to make the world a better place. He knew that if people, especially teenagers, had someone to talk to, they could always choose a better path.

He started weekly socials at the community center. Now people could get together to play sports, play boardgames, or just talk.

With a full-time income in his network marketing business, Andy had plenty of time to expand his contributions. Next came the local suicide prevention hotline. Andy plans more projects. He feels fulfillment every hour of every day by helping others. All of this was possible with his free time and residual income.

Frank's story.

Everyone says they wish they could volunteer more. But we all have limits. Other obligations are always in our way. The biggest time obligation most people have? A job.

Frank is all about giving back. The more money he earned in his business, the bigger percentage he could give back to his favorite causes. As a part-time network marketer, he finally was able to drop his second job. This gave Frank the time he needed to devote his personal efforts to worthy causes. Plus, he met new prospects while volunteering his time.

What about Frank's network marketing team? Many of them started volunteering also. They saw their network marketing business was not only about money, but also a vehicle that gave them options to do more with their lives.

THE BLUE PERSONALITY.

Did the yellow personality not describe us? Let's talk about the next personality, the blue personality. The best way to remember the blue personality is to think of the word, "fun."

Blue personalities love to party, travel, experience unique adventures, see new things, and would love a 24-hour-a-day social life. Blue personalities are easy to recognize because they are always talking. Look for someone with a lot of energy, a short attention span, and a very active life.

Because of their view of the world, we will find many blue personalities in professions such as:

- Sales.
- Public relations.
- The travel industry.
- Hospitality.
- Bartending.

Do we know someone who talks a lot? Do we know someone with endless energy? How about that tour guide that never stopped talking? Or that cousin who always has a new story to tell?

Do we need more help visualizing a blue personality?

How about the cartoon character SpongeBob SquarePants? Or Bugs Bunny? Short attention span, endless energy, and excited about life.

But what about goals for blue personalities?

Do we still have a picture of a blue personality in our minds? How would that person want to meet new people? What activity would that person naturally enjoy? Here are some examples:

- Organizing a group of friends for a weekend trip.
- Traveling and seeing new things three weeks out of the month.
- A chance to speak to a group, any group.
- Going to events and meeting new people.
- Having a bucket list of exciting things to experience.

These would be typical blue personality goals.

What goals would not be in alignment?

Could you imagine a blue personality wanting these goals?

- A quiet day at home reading a book.
- A boring job as a night watchman.
- Sitting at a computer monitoring and calculating his or her investment returns.
- Spending hours organizing a collection of miniature art.

These goals would be sheer torture to the blue personality. They want to live. They want to experience. They want to have fun.

GOAL-SETTING FOR BLUE PERSONALITIES.

Again, our goal will be to meet new people for our network marketing business. With this be hard for blue personalities? Not at all! Meeting new people is natural for blue personalities. Any activity that involves other people will be natural and fun.

Unlike some personalities, blue personalities want action. They don't want to waste time planning and measuring their accomplishments. Paperwork and statistics are for other people to worry about.

Let's take a quick look at a typical blue personality's activities and mini-goals. Remember, the goal is to meet new people. These activities will help achieve that goal.

Tim's story.

Every morning Tim asks himself, "Who can I talk to? I am ready to have some fun! Bring on the action!"

Tim is all energy. You get motivated just by hanging out with him. He loves to have fun and he loves to talk.

No one is a stranger; if they make eye contact, he assumes they want to talk to him. His network marketing business suits his personality perfectly. He gets to talk to everyone, and I mean **everyone**. He tries to be in a group of people constantly.

What makes Tim a pro? Instead of talking "at" people, he learned to ask questions. Getting others engaged in the conversation is key. No one wants to listen to a Tim monologue.

What kind of activities will Tim find for his goal of meeting new, interesting people? Here are a few things that Tim would do:

- Organic vegan cooking club? Tim likes steak, but thought it would be fun to try a new diet.

- Sci-fi book club? The story would be interesting, but not nearly as interesting as talking to other book club members about the story.

- Free accounting classes at the library? This was a big stretch. Tim never made it to the second class. But, he got to talk to other personalities that were extreme introverts. It was a chance to meet new people with a different point of view.

- A dog-walking group? Why not? Tim didn't have a dog, but he could borrow one. Dog walkers were a captive audience for Tim. Great conversations while walking in the park or watching the dogs exercise. And what do the other dog owners want to talk about? Yes, they love talking about their dogs.

- Neighborhood gatherings? Everybody loves the grill master. Tim wouldn't grill burgers. Too boring. He would grill more exotic items that attracted people to his grill. Instant conversation!

- Discount coupons? Anything can be an excuse for a blue personality to start a group. Tim watched for discount coupons for new restaurants, and would then organize an impromptu dinner club. Discount coupons for entertainment and amusement parks were even more fun. Not only did Tim get to meet more people in the group, he also had a fun day of entertainment. Painting, skydiving, local tours, exercise classes, concert tickets, the possibilities are endless.

- And Tim naturally said, "Yes." Have you ever seen the *Yes Man* movie? The 2008 movie's main character was played by Jim Carrey. The character was an uptight, business-only personality. He was hypnotized to say "yes" to every question. He learned a new foreign language. He learned how to fly a plane. Everything people asked him to do, he had to say "yes." He transformed into a blue personality because he realized how much fun he missed in his formerly structured, all-business life. A "yes man" will meet hundreds of new people.

Remember the big goal?

It was to meet new people. Look at the fun activities Tim does to reach that goal.

Is every day a great day for Tim? Yes!

Tim doesn't need a motivational pep talk in the morning. He doesn't need extra incentives to overcome his fears. Tim's activities are natural for him, within his comfort zone.

We have no fear, only fun, when our activities fit our color personality. Our journey to our goal is easy, natural, and enjoyable.

Creating activities to meet new people is natural and easy for blue personalities. But, what about other goals that blue personalities desire?

MORE GOALS FOR BLUE PERSONALITIES.

Meeting new people is great. Blue personalities love this activity. But, what other goals can we achieve as blue personalities with our network marketing income? Let's expand our options.

The partying grandparents.

Wanting to retire early, Marty and Sally knew what they wanted out of their business. Sure, the full-time income was nice, but what they really wanted was to spend time with their grandkids. And, they wanted to kick that goal into high gear.

Their local climate allowed "swimming pool season" to be six months out of the year. Why not have a pool, but make it the best pool ever?

Instead of steps, they designed a walk-in entrance so all kids, of all ages and all abilities, could safely get into the water.

A waterslide? Not just any ordinary waterslide. Their pool had a giant waterslide that could accommodate inner tubes.

Two diving boards. One regular board and of course, a high-dive board for the adventurous adrenaline-fueled teenagers.

How deep was the deep end of their swimming pool? Deep enough so they could teach and scuba-certify their grandchildren.

Marty and Sally's house became Party Central, and the grandkids always looked forward to their visits. Pool time was quality time for bonding and fun.

The traveling duo.

Bob and Jana? They were made for travel. After the kids were out of the house, they knew it was time. Sell the house. Trade the car for a motorcycle. Buy an RV. Get ready to visit their downline across the country.

In between visiting their team members, they would find their next adventure.

- Stopping at all the amusement parks with top-rated roller coasters.
- Touring all the national parks.
- Traveling the entire Pacific Coast Highway.
- Attending Motorcycle Week in Florida.
- Enjoying music festivals.
- Skydiving in every state they visited.
- Visiting their kids in university to attend the football games.

And what was even better?

Every place they went, the locals would recommend the newest hidden adventure. Never a dull day for Bob and Jana! Their motto? "Keep those network marketing bonus checks coming."

THE RED PERSONALITY.

Now, if the yellow and blue personalities did not feel natural to us, maybe we are a red personality. Red personalities find happiness in achievement, recognition, and having power and money.

Many top athletes are red personalities. They don't run a race for fun. And, they won't slow down so somebody else can have the satisfaction of winning. They compete against others, and they compete against themselves. Red personalities are bottom-line people. They measure everything in results.

Because of their view of the world, we find red personalities in professions such as:

- Politics. Yes, elect me, so I can tell you what to do.
- Managers and bosses.
- Organizers.

Do we know someone who wants to take charge? Someone who wants to get things organized and get the project moving? People that can stay ultra-focused to get the results they want?

Do we need a little help visualizing a red personality?

Presidents, prime ministers, record-setting athletes, and the neighbor that desperately wants to be the president of the local volunteer school board. Or competitive salespeople, board of education organizers, and people who set deadlines for everything.

What kinds of goals do red personalities want?

When we think of power, achievement, and being in charge, these would be natural examples of red personality goals:

- To win the local election.
- To be elected to the board of directors' hall of fame.
- To organize the community fundraising event so it raises enough money to build that hospital.
- To accumulate the biggest investment portfolio among his or her friends.
- To have the newest, fastest, most desired car with personalized license plates.

What goals would not be in alignment?

Could you imagine a red personality wanting these goals?

- To take a quiet, scenic holiday on a deserted island?
- To spend hours at a party chitchatting about local gossip?
- To have an extra 30 minutes every day for quiet meditation and contemplation?
- To take up quilting?

Of course not. Red personalities want to measure their success and beat their previous records.

Goal-setting for red personalities.

Meeting people is never an issue for red personalities. They are not shy! Reds have the answers to everyone's problems, and won't hesitate to tell other people exactly what they should do.

If meeting new people was a numbers game, the red personalities would want to win it. And even though meeting new people isn't a game, the red personalities keep a scorecard. They will compete with themselves!

Mandy's story.

Competitive and driven, Mandy is ready to take on the world. She loves challenges and measures her performance by winning. As the top achiever in her high school, she made sure she graduated in record time at her university.

What can Mandy do with her knowledge? Once a week, she and her coworkers go to the local bar and compete in trivia competitions. This means every week she meets at least 10 new people. Not content with only one night a week, Mandy organizes additional trivia competitions during her business travels.

Mandy looks for higher mental stimulation at the free academic lectures at the local university. Here she meets like-minded people who want to learn and understand new things. Their deep conversations build connections among the group.

Mandy jumps out of bed every morning, anxious to take on the newest challenge of her day. She makes sure her challenges include contact with new people. Every day is a great day for Mandy.

David's story.

David doesn't believe in patience. Direct and to the point, he wants people to know his intention is to build his business … now. Every event and encounter includes a direct request to check out his business.

Since David is single, he decided to try speed-dating. Fortunately, he was direct and honest with every speed-dating participant. He would say, "I am super busy. Let me be frank. If we are compatible as a couple, you won't see much of me. I am working hard on my business for the future."

Yes, a bit forward, but at least David was honest.

Did David turn off some participants? Yes.

Did some participants go on a date with David because he was a go-getter? Yes.

Did some of the prospects decline a date, but ask about his business? Yes.

Did David eventually find a compatible match? Yes. It was a good prospecting system while it lasted.

Does David need motivation in the morning? No. David can't wait to see the first person of the day to tell him or her about his business. David loves his business, and he loves talking about his business with others.

Red personalities constantly measure their direct results. They hate investing time in social chit-chat. They focus their activities to get the best possible result for their time invested.

To reach their lofty goals, their interactions are more transactional than relational. Red personalities find satisfaction by keeping score of their accomplishments.

MORE GOALS FOR RED PERSONALITIES.

Meeting new people is great. Red personalities have less fear of rejection, and feel motivated by their personal achievements. But are their goals limited to reaching the top level in their network marketing businesses? Of course not. They use their network marketing income and skills to continue growing in all areas of their lives.

Real estate.

As a red personality, Doris loves investments where she is in control. No passive investments for her. That is why Doris loves to invest in real estate.

She knew her hometown in Florida is an attractive destination for people looking to retire. So what was her strategy?

Doris took her business income and approached the local realtor. She offered to buy available houses quickly if they offered a discount. Doris didn't need to worry about financing. Her financial statement was strong.

Since houses in her area languished in estates and the heirs wanted to settle quickly, Doris acquired houses at great prices.

Next, Doris approached a different realtor who specialized in helping retirees find their next home. Her residual income meant she could wait for a favorable sale price.

As soon as Doris sold a home, she bought the next one. Her real estate empire grew. She loves being in charge of her investments. No hands-off mutual funds for her. She loves being in charge of her asset portfolio.

Youth soccer.

Harry was a star in his high school soccer days. Reliving those memories felt good.

So as soon as Harry's little boy could walk, Harry organized a toddler's soccer league. He put together the league's schedule, appointed the league's statistician, and scheduled the league's draft.

Guess who was the coach of his son's team?

Harry, of course. Red personalities get things done. From planning to execution, Harry made sure the toddler league moved forward.

And did Harry enjoy the project? Of course. He graphed and charted everything from start to finish.

And was this a great way to meet other parents? Yes. Everyone knew Harry and respected him for what he accomplished.

The band that made the school proud.

When Anne's daughter joined the junior high band, she immediately took action. Why should her daughter have daily boring band practices in the school's gymnasium? Not this band. This band is going to perform!

Anne raised money for uniforms. Next, she scheduled band performances for holidays and events. She even convinced the school to bus the band to other school districts. Now they could play head-to-head in special competitions.

Did the other band members benefit from this upgraded school band experience? Yes! And they loved the trophies too.

But guess who now knows every band member's parents? Anne, of course. She met new people while helping the school band set new standards.

THE GREEN PERSONALITY.

Well, if the yellow, blue, and red personalities did not feel natural to us, maybe we are a green personality. What are some traits of green personalities? They find happiness in facts, figures, research and the security of having all the information.

Green personalities take time to make decisions. They want to explore the different possibilities, and assess the risks or dangers of a decision. And yes, green personalities like to be right. The absence of information creates stress.

Because this is how they see the world, we will find green personalities in professions such as:

- Accounting.
- Science.
- Computer technology.
- Engineering.

Green personalities are more comfortable with books and computers. Social interaction is not a natural trait. Green personalities are the opposite of the outgoing and impulsive blue personalities.

Do you know people who are cautious? Who take the time to get all the facts? People who want to feel secure about what they do? Think the word, "safety."

Want some examples of green personalities to keep in your mind?

Imagine that student from high school who got perfect scores in physics, chemistry, and mathematics. Or think about the person who invested months in designing the suspension bridge over the river. The desire for knowledge would be key in determining if we were a green personality.

What types of goals would green personalities have?

Here is a sample list:

- To get a home in a nice neighborhood with an attractive mortgage interest rate.
- To save more than they spend.
- To have an economical car that gets great gas mileage.
- To never have to worry about debt or money.
- To chart their net worth and watch it grow.
- To have clothes and shoes that last a long time so they don't have to buy more.
- To purchase assets at an inexpensive price and watch them appreciate.

What goals would not be in alignment?

Could you imagine a green personality with these goals?

- A hippie lifestyle, traveling with hand-to-mouth finances.

- Buying depreciating assets like a new car every year.

- A party lifestyle with shallow conversations with strangers.

Of course not. Security is high on their list. Plus, spur-of-the-moment decisions are uncomfortable.

Goal-setting for green personalities.

Remember our goal for this exercise? It is to meet new people for our network marketing business. Of all the personalities, this is the most challenging for the green personalities.

But the good news? It is not impossible. Green personalities should arrange activities that are within their comfort zones. Then they will consistently meet and interact with new people.

Let's look at how green personalities reach this goal.

Erica's story.

As an accountant, Erica doesn't often meet new people at her job. But her skills at mathematics helped her discover that she loves brewing beer at home. It is a fun hobby, and she loves testing the reactions of different raw ingredients.

But what can she do with all that beer? No problem. Erica learned that she was an instant celebrity when people found out about her hobby. She didn't have to reach out to other people. People loved to invite her to parties and social gatherings. They encouraged her to bring samples of her latest batch of beer. That gave Erica something to talk about.

Because of her obsession with home-brewing, Erica discovered the local home-brewing club. Here she met like-minded enthusiasts. They spent hours discussing the nuances of their craft. New friends were easy to come by. They had so much in common and talking was easy and stress-free. Maybe the beer helped!

Now Erica looks forward to the meetings and actively seeks out new clubs.

Brian's story.

Brian spent his office hours in a cubicle as a video editor. It was the perfect job for his shy personality. Networking would never happen at his office. But what do shy people have as their advantage?

They are great listeners. People love listeners. Brian found it easier to listen while others talked. He only had to talk when other people asked him questions. Not so bad.

While Brian was a huge sports fan, he wasn't much of a participant. Of course he needed exercise, but running seemed so competitive. He searched through the local groups in his community and found a walking club. They met six times a week, twice a day. That gave anyone the opportunity to participate no matter what their weekly schedule was like.

Walking was easy. The participants loved new members. Yes, someone else they could talk to.

Brian perfected his listening skills, learned to ask interesting questions, and was soon the most popular member of the group. Everyone wanted to walk with Brian.

Some members were lonely. Some wanted to lose weight. And some members participated just to stay active.

This was the perfect opportunity for Brian to meet someone new. Since Brian sold weight-loss products, connecting with new customers and potential distributors was easy.

His formula? Walk, listen, and if someone wanted to lose weight, let them know that he had a solution.

Walking was easy and within Brian's comfort zone. He looked forward to his daily walks. Relaxing, casual conversation that helped build his business.

What else can green personalities do to meet people?

Social media is great. It is available 24 hours a day, and people don't have to leave their homes. If the interaction gets too intense, all one has to do is walk away from the computer. So for green personalities, this is the perfect place for them to expand their interaction with people.

With simple search queries, green personalities can locate new people to converse with, such as:

- People with common careers.
- People with common interests and hobbies.
- People who live in the same area.
- Former classmates.
- Foodies with the same eclectic tastes.
- Boardgame enthusiasts.

- Travel junkies.

- Sports fanatics.

- People who love the same genre of movies.

While green personalities are not natural socializers, they can connect with people in comfortable, controlled environments. It may take a little imagination to do this, but the green personalities are happy with the consistent results.

MORE GOALS FOR GREEN PERSONALITIES.

Meeting new people builds our business. But, what else can we do now that we have time and money freedom from our network marketing business? Where can we go from here?

Cautious and planned.

Inspired by the book, *The Millionaire Next Door*, Robbie became a follower of the "quiet" wealthy. These millionaires quietly accumulate wealth, yet never flash their wealth for others to see.

What was the most popular car for these millionaires? A pickup truck. So Robbie had to get a pickup truck.

Every financial decision followed a checklist to ensure that it was a smart decision. No monetary decisions were made on a whim. Everything was planned out to the penny. And of course, there was a scientific balance between cash and liquid assets in Robbie's long-term financial planning.

Did Robbie quit his job after his bonus checks surpassed his salary? Not a chance. Why throw away a 100% raise? Plus, Robbie's full-time career was a great way to meet new people for his network marketing business.

Robbie lives off of 50% of his income. He invests the other 50% of his income in ways that make his accountant drool.

Addicted to learning.

Even after multiple degrees from graduate school, Bert still loves to learn. His goal is to learn something new every day. Bert's full-time income in network marketing means more free time to continue his passion as a professional student.

Bert wanted to learn how to cook. So, he applied to culinary school. He wanted to save money on his taxes, so he took a business accounting class at night school.

Next Bert wondered what it would take to open up a new restaurant. That meant a restaurant management course.

With his new skills, Bert reached for his dream and opened his own restaurant. The banquet room became the new weekly meeting location for his growing network marketing group.

Is opening a restaurant everyone's dream? No. But it was Bert's dream, and his network marketing business made it possible.

BUT WHY SO LITTLE MENTION OF SOCIAL MEDIA?

Social media is one more way to meet people. The key is to meet people in a way that is natural for us.

So yes, social media is a way to meet people, but it isn't the only way. Is it an appropriate way for us?

One way to understand this is to ask this question:

Why do people go on social media?

1. We like to be informed. We want to know what is going on in our world. This could mean keeping up with our friends. Or, we may research a hobby or interest. Of course we can do much of this research during work hours when we should be working.

2. We want entertainment. Who doesn't? We love leaving our current reality and immersing ourselves in movies, pictures, and stories. Social media provides this entertainment on-demand. For example:

- A cat waterskiing? We better watch the whole video.

- 11 juicy secrets we didn't know about a popular movie star that we will never meet. Let's read that list now.

- Take this quiz to find out which dessert matches our lifestyle. Oh, let me share this gem with my friends!

3. We want an active virtual social life. It is easy to have hundreds of imaginary close friends around the world that we connect with. Who wouldn't love to have a good friend in Laos? Definitely something to talk about with our other friends that we've never met in person.

Notice something missing?

Yes. We don't go on social media to read blatant advertising from our friends ... or from strangers. We want our social news feed to be ... news!

What happens when we advertise and push our products and opportunity on our friends? It is like asking them not to watch or follow us anymore.

People hate a hard sell. But the fun fact is that people love to buy.

We do want to talk about our business when appropriate, right? It is easier to talk to friends than strangers, so social media gives us the chance to make more friends.

Our focus should be to continue meeting and connecting with people. When the time is appropriate, when our friend has a problem that we can help with, then we can mention our business solution. But this comes from being a friend and listening. Chances are it won't happen from a generic advertisement about our product or opportunity.

More about using social media.

Social media isn't only for green personalities. Any of the personalities could use the following tips to connect with more people.

It isn't the medium we use that makes the difference. It is our sincere and authentic connections with people that count.

So it doesn't matter if we connect with John via social media, by having lunch, by saying "hi" in the grocery store, or attending a conference. John is still the same person no matter the method we used to connect.

Haven't really connected with anyone on your social media friends list?

We can connect with five friends a day by private message. Here are some possibilities if we don't know how to start.

1. Bringing up our common ground. We could say that we are:

- Catching up with some of our school classmates.
- Catching up with some of the people we used to work with.
- Connecting with friends from last year's soccer season.

2. Asking them what they do at their job. We could say:

- "I am just curious, I see you are working at the gas company. What exactly do you do there?"

- "I noticed you didn't list your occupation on your profile. I am just curious, what do you do for a living now? Did you change careers?"

3. Prepare a great answer when they ask what we do now. Our answer could pre-qualify them as an interested prospect. We could say:

- "I am still teaching, but I also started a part-time business helping people save on their electric bills."

- "I quit my job and started a business from my home. I hated the commuting."

- "I got bored as an accountant, so I started a part-time skincare business from my home."

Social media is connecting with people.

There are plenty of detailed courses on using social media. But we have to ask ourselves if this is the way we wish to meet new people for our business. Maybe it is. What if the only time we have for meeting new people is after 11 PM, when the family is asleep? Then, social media is better than meeting drunks in the local tavern.

There are always people to meet.

People are everywhere. Depending on our color personality, we want to meet people in a way that suits our style.

And what if we are introverts and are reluctant to approach people? No problem. Here is one solution.

Talk to people who have to talk to you.

Every day we meet people who get paid to talk to us. Who are these people? Anyone with a job that has to ask us a question.

How many of the following people do we meet every week?

- Coffee shop baristas.
- Waiters.
- Managers.
- Hostesses.
- Retail sales clerks.
- Gas stations attendants.

We continually meet these people while out and about.

Talking to these people throughout our week can create a big list of new prospects. The good news for introverted personalities? They don't have to start the conversation. These people are paid to start the conversations.

WHAT IF WE ARE NOT SURE OF OUR COLOR PERSONALITY?

Don't worry. These personalities are not chiseled in stone. They are only guidelines to help us understand who we are.

A simple three-question test.

Forget about money or time limitations. Write down the first answers that come to mind.

Question #1. On your days off from work, what do you like to do?

Question #2. On vacation, where do you like to go?

Question #3. When you retire, what would you like to do?

That was a very short test.

Our answers should help guide us to our color personality.

We might think, "I think I am a little bit blue and a little bit yellow." That is okay. This means that we will feel good about goals that are natural to both of these color personalities.

Are we still unsure? Then ask our friends what color personality they think we are. They might be able to help, since we are biased in how we see ourselves.

Still don't know what color personality we are? Here are three explanations for that:

#1. We are a yellow personality and want others to tell us the color we should be to make them happy.

#2. We are a blue personality and there are other things that are more fun than thinking about this.

#3. We are a green personality and need more data to study before we make our final decision.

Okay, just kidding about these explanations.

What about red personalities? They know who they are. No confusion there.

The point to remember is this: different personalities have different goals. What we want in our lives may not be what others want in their lives.

But what about that second factor we mentioned earlier in this book?

Choosing goals that are in alignment with our color personality is only the first step.

It is time to move on to the second step, our individual values. If we know which values are important to us, we can choose goals that are in alignment with these values. This eliminates conflicting feelings when we try to reach a goal that doesn't match our values.

Factor #2:
What are our values?

Values help us decide what is important to us in life. We have to make choices. We can't do everything simultaneously. So how do we choose what we will do at any particular moment?

By choosing the tasks that are in alignment with our highest values. Let's look at an example.

As a high school student, I had homework. One of my values was to get a good education. But, I also loved music and playing the drums. As a teenager, which value do you think was higher in my mind? Yes, I spent many more hours playing the drums than doing my homework. I made that choice based upon my values.

Let's move forward 20 years. My values changed. Now it is more important for my daughter to have a quiet environment for sleeping than for me to be playing my drums. Again, this is a decision based upon my values.

Values are guidelines. Sometimes we have to do a task of a lower value because it is urgent at the moment. But, we will be looking at the big picture in this book. When we set our goals, we want them based on our higher values. We want our goals to help us reach the things we want in our lives.

Let's dive into the values now. First, we will describe the values. Then, we will look at which color personalities feel attracted to individual values.

These are not the only values in life. This list is good enough for now. You can always add or subtract different values and create your own customized list.

The 14 values.

As we cover the following 14 values, think about which of the values are most important to you. When we are through describing the values, we can rank these values by how important they are to us.

No need to rank the values now. Just be aware that this will be our next step. And at the end of the description of each value, we will mention which color personality would have that value.

This is only a quick summary of the values, but let's get started.

Value # 1: Power.

People with this value:

- Like to be in charge.
- Are always right, and others are wrong.
- Need everything to be perfect.
- Crave control.
- Want the final say.
- Have the mindset of, "If we are not first, we're last."
- Will often think, "Don't tell me what to do!"

- Have two rules. Rule #1: I am right. Rule #2: If you disagree, see Rule #1.
- Won't want to give up or give in.
- Play the hardest to win, even at boardgames.
- Will activate self-motivation instantly if challenged.

This value is common with red personalities.

Value #2: Financial security.

People with this value:

- Are thrifty.
- Are responsible with money.
- Know their account balances to the penny.
- Reduce any risk for everything in their lives.
- Focus on saving money versus spending money.
- Do math in their sleep.
- Save any raise they get.
- Worry and plan for the future.
- Spend less, invest more.
- Look for bargains, discounts, and safe investments.

This value is common with green personalities and some yellow personalities.

Value #3: Desire to be rich.

People with this value:

- Want to look good and impressive.
- Want the best and want people to notice when they have it.
- Think that if the credit card isn't maxed out, there is room to spend.
- Post pictures of their success on social media.
- Use a money clip attached to their credit cards so they can flash a $100 bill on the outside.
- Take care of their assets.

This value is common with red personalities and some blue personalities.

Value #4: Desire to look good.

People with this value:

- Will not leave the house without their hair styled or makeup applied.
- Watch what they eat.
- Make time at the gym a priority.
- Don't feel good if they don't look good.
- Could spend hours choosing an outfit.
- Have more shoes than days of the month.
- Spend more on vanity products than on the mortgage.
- Won't go jogging without makeup.
- Know what label they are wearing and hope that others notice.

This value is common with red personalities and some blue personalities.

Value #5: Loving relationship with a partner.

People with this value:

- Think about their partner constantly.
- Talk and share with their partner often.
- Make decisions based upon their partner's wants.
- Go out as a couple with few exceptions.
- Know that quality time is a priority.
- Text their partner during work to say hello.
- Will buy small gifts "just because."
- Spend time planning every holiday and day off to make it special for their partner.
- Wear matching shirts on vacations and weekend trips.

This value is very common with yellow personalities.

Value #6: Family.

People with this value:

- Don't miss family functions.
- Are active and supportive of every committee or PTA group for their kids.
- Plan the reunions and make sure everyone feels involved.

- Know when to shut off work and spend time with the family.
- Are known as the "hostess with the mostest."
- Have a minivan that looks like a children's playground inside.
- Include kids and pets in all activities, and sometimes the neighbors' kids and pets too.
- Respond to anyone who shouts "Mom" or "Dad" in a public place.

This value is common with yellow personalities.

Value #7: Career fulfillment.

People with this value:

- Want to reach the top of the career ladder.
- Think about work all the time, even as they sleep.
- Think that vacation is a time to plan for career advancement, not relax.
- Spend more time at the office to feel successful.
- Work on the drive to and from the office.
- Demand 6 AM "get pumped" conference calls.
- Are go-getters.
- Have five cups of coffee before 9 AM.
- Dress two levels up from their pay scale.
- Love to hear that they are hard workers.
- Can talk business 24/7.

- Have automatic self-motivation.

This value is common with red personalities and some blue personalities.

Value #8: Desire to feel needed.

People with this value:

- Want to be indispensable.
- Are busy being busy.
- Volunteer for everything, even if they are not asked.
- Have loyalty as a top priority.
- Always want to help.
- Don't think about themselves.
- Put others first.
- Are involved with fundraisers, social work, community projects, and charitable activities.

This value is common with yellow personalities.

Value #9: Personal enlightenment.

People with this value:

- Enjoy thinking about thinking.
- Find that the deeper the philosophy, the more intriguing it is.
- Think outside of the box.
- Love to share knowledge of findings and discoveries.
- Ponder the meaning of everything.

- Are non-confrontational and allow others to have different viewpoints.
- Want to feel that everything can have a higher purpose.

This value is common with green personalities and yellow personalities.

Value #10: Adventure junkie.

People with this value:

- Daydream about the next adventure.
- Are ready to travel at a moment's notice.
- Are the first to take a risk in everything.
- Can become completely obsessed with ideas that they love.
- Are always up for the next challenge.
- Think adrenaline is an essential nutrient.
- Are of the opinion that the more dangerous the adventure, the better.
- Can't imagine why they would sleep when there are adventures to be had.
- Frequently say, "Watch this!" Or, "Let's do this now!"
- Circle the next big experience on their calendars.

This value is very common with blue personalities.

Value #11: Aim for fame.

People with this value:

- Drop names of people they know or want to know.
- Refer to famous people as friends, even if they only saw a passing glimpse of them in a crowd.
- Want everyone to know how important they are.
- Will post pictures on social media of themselves with anyone famous.
- Think that every picture on social media should be about them.
- "I" and "me" are their favorite names.
- Love to be story-toppers.
- Think their status is as essential as oxygen.
- Are the first to be on the VIP list of the new restaurant in town.
- Crave attention and recognition.

This value is common with red personalities and sometimes blue personalities.

Value #12: Popularity.

People with this value:

- Want everybody to know their name.
- Want everybody to consider them their friend.
- Have friends from all walks of life.
- Want strangers to like them.

- Want to feel good about what others think of them.
- Will be the last to leave the room.
- Circulate in groups until they meet everyone.
- Are energized by the approval of others.

This value is common with yellow and blue personalities, and some red personalities.

Value #13: Accomplishments.

People with this value:

- Set ten-year goals. Then twenty-year goals.
- Set daily goals.
- Set hourly goals, and record their progress.
- Will strive for the award, trophy, and recognition.
- Will talk to anyone if it helps their goal.
- Will do their best not to fail.
- Are happy to share their personal vision.
- Get offended when others don't ask them about their lives.
- Will get the job done.
- Won't give up.

This value is common with red personalities, and some green and blue personalities as well.

Value #14: Desire to have a good time.

People with this value:

- Focus on having fun no matter what the occasion.

- Will often make boring things exciting.

- Are having fun when they're not working. Sometimes even when they **are** working.

- Are extremely social so that they can find new friends.

- Love to do things in a group, or enjoy finding a new group.

- Are not self-conscious.

- Are always entertaining.

- Love talking about themselves or telling stories.

- Can't imagine why they'd stay at home when they could be having fun someplace else.

- Love networking groups, clubs, team sports, and activities that involve other people.

- Are first in the conga dance line.

This value? Common with blue personalities, of course.

Can we add more?

Sure.

Are some of these values exaggerated? Yes.

Do all of us possess a little of each value? Of course.

So we don't want to be judgmental about these values. We only want to know which values motivate us more … or less.

Which values are most important to us?

Yikes! With 14 different values, how do we know which values to put first? We could spend hours or days working on this.

Here is a shortcut. Take 14 index cards or pieces of paper. Write one value on each card. Then put the cards on a table. We are going to arrange the cards by importance.

This is the fastest way to sort the cards. Take two cards. Quickly make a decision which card value is more important. That card will go on top. Then take the next card, and see where that card fits in. It is always easier to make a choice between two cards than it is to choose from all 14 at once.

Now we have a general idea of which values are the most important to us. This doesn't have to be 100% accurate. What we want to know is generally what is more important to us.

We want our goals to be about our top values. If our goals are about the lower values, we won't have the motivation to work in these uninteresting areas of our lives. This means that we will procrastinate, get frustrated, and fail. If we are going to work on our goals, let's work on goals that we feel great about and that match our values.

What will our top-priority goals be?

Let me give you some examples.

Our friend, Mike, is an adventure junkie. He likes personal enlightenment and trying new things. Security is very low on his list of priorities. If Mike were to set goals about security, he would be bored and uninspired. Every day would be a struggle. There would be no natural motivation. For Mike, picking a goal about security would be a recipe for massive failure.

Our other friend, Sandy, has different values as her priorities. Financial security and career accomplishment make her eyes light up. If she were to set her goals in these areas, every day she would enjoy the journey to her goal fulfillment.

Our friend Ed is quite different. His priorities? Family and a loving relationship with his partner. If he were to set goals for nonstop travel or to be popular, he would quickly abandon these goals. We want our internal inspiration to motivate and drive us. That is why picking the right goal for us is necessary.

Take the time now to sort the cards.

We might even get a smile on our faces as we realize who we are by how we sort our cards.

DREAM-BUILDING IS WISHING AND HOPING.

Yes, wishing and hoping won't get results, but they are a necessary first step.

Unless we have a dream, something we have passion for, we won't feel good about attempting our goals. So we definitely will do some dream-building.

However, we won't stop there. There is more.

What if we pick the wrong goal?

What if we pick an exciting goal, but it doesn't match our values?

What if we pick a goal that will be difficult for our personality to execute?

What if we pick a goal that we don't have enough passion for?

What if we pick a goal that is doomed to failure?

But what if …

What if we pick the right goal?

What if we pick a goal that feels congruent with our personal values?

What if we pick a goal that feels easy to accomplish?

What if we pick a goal that naturally motivates us every morning?

As we can see, picking the correct goal for our personality and values is 90% of our success.

In the past, we may have picked goals that didn't match our personality or values exactly, so those goals felt difficult.

Let's take a look at the four steps we will need to follow to choose the correct goal for us.

THE FOUR MAGIC STEPS TO ACHIEVING OUR GOAL.

If we follow these four magic steps, we are 90% of the way to achieving our goal!

Yes, as we saw in the last chapter, picking the correct goal is the magic that makes things happen.

So let's look at these four steps, and then we will discuss them one by one.

Step #1: Dream. Pick the goal of our dreams.

Step #2: Check if this goal matches our personality type.

Step #3: Check if this goal is in line with our values.

Step #4: Find a mini-habit that will make achieving this goal automatic.

That is it. Not too hard. When we follow these four steps, here is what happens:

- We feel natural internal motivation every day.
- We never have mixed feelings about the direction of our lives.
- Every day is a fun day as we enjoy the journey to our goal.

- The mini-habit assures us that we are making progress every day.

Wow! Now we have a real goal, a real direction in our lives.

This might explain why we have struggled with goals before. If we don't take each step into consideration, our goals are destined for failure.

Let's discuss the first three steps. We'll discuss the fourth step, mini-habits, in the next chapter.

Step #1: Dream. Pick the goal of our dreams.

This is the "wishing and hoping" step. "Wishing and hoping" are not enough to achieve a goal, but it is the start. Here we choose the goal we want to accomplish.

Do we have to attend a goal-setting seminar to choose our goal? Of course not. But, we may get new ideas or get inspired by others at the seminar. Or, reading an inspirational book about someone's life may help us choose our goal.

So Step #1 is choosing our initial goal.

Don't worry if this is the right goal for us or not. This is only the "wishing and hoping" first step.

Once we choose our goal, we will check if it can stand up to our personality type, and if it is congruent with our values. If our goal doesn't pass meet both of these criteria, that is a sign that we should modify our goal or choose a different one.

So for now, let's pick a goal.

For an example, we will choose a goal to:

"Retire from our job and spend more time educating teenagers on personal finances."

Step #2: Check if this goal matches our personality type.

For this example, we will be a yellow personality.

Does this goal match our personality type? Our goal is to:

"Retire from our job and spend more time educating teenagers on personal finances."

Yes, this is very much a yellow personality goal. As yellow personalities, we find happiness in helping others.

But, what if we were a blue personality? Attention to detail and boring personal finances may not be the passion of our lives.

What if we were a red personality? Well, retiring from our job so we could be our own boss would be exciting. But would we feel passionate about volunteering our time teaching teenagers about personal finances? We might want something else. Maybe we would want a goal that had more personal recognition, or a goal that could be measured in dollars and cents.

So if we were a blue personality or a red personality, we should go back and modify our goal. This would not be the goal that gives us our internal motivation every morning.

But what about a green personality? Retiring from the security of a job? Well, it would make sense if our network marketing income felt secure. Teaching teenagers about personal finances? Yes, we would enjoy outlining the course in exquisite detail. So for a green personality, this might pass the personality type requirement for our goal.

Step #3: Check if this goal is in line with our values.

Remember Value #8: Desire to feel needed? If we were a yellow personality, that would be near the top of our list of values. Here is a review of the main points.

People with this value:

- Want to be indispensable.
- Are busy being busy.
- Are volunteers extraordinaire.
- Are loyal.
- Always want to help.

Yes, yellow personalities find fulfillment and happiness when this value is used in goal-setting. So helping teenagers understand personal finance feels good and natural.

For a yellow personality, this goal passes the test. This goal matches the personality type, and the values.

Now, that wasn't very hard, was it?

Take a moment now to wish, hope, and choose your personal goal.

Then, check if that goal matches your personality type and your values.

Once you have a goal that you feel good about, all we have left is the last step. In the next chapter, we will learn how to create a mini-habit that will make achieving that goal fun and automatic.

Step #4: Mini-habits.

Start small.

We have to build our goal-achieving muscles. Little victories with small goals give us the confidence to achieve larger goals. So in the beginning, let's start with something simple.

1. Have a short time limit for our goal. One week, two weeks, or even four weeks. As humans, we have short attention spans. It is too easy to fall back into our day-to-day habits and forget our new goals. A shorter time frame will help us keep focused.

For example, it is hard for us to visualize making a goal of thirteen million continuous breaths over a period of years. Instead, it is easier to concentrate on meeting the immediate goal of our next breath.

2. Make our goal small. We don't start off our running career with a 26-mile marathon. When I decided to run a marathon, I started running only one mile at a time. I could do that. It was a small victory for me.

After my body adjusted to running one mile, I started running two miles at a time, and so on. Finally, after months of daily training, I entered and finished my first marathon.

It is the same with goals. With a small goal, we can achieve it quickly. Little victories give us confidence.

3. Make sure our goal fits our personality style. If we are a green personality, we are not as outgoing or social as others. To set a goal of talking to 30 new people a day would be disastrous. We would feel uncomfortable. We would dread working on our goal. Our motivation would be at an all-time low.

4. Make sure our new and smaller goal is in alignment with our values. When our goals and values match, motivation is automatic. We won't need mental tricks to get us excited about our goals. If our goals are not in alignment with our values, we will feel like we are lying to ourselves.

And now on to our mini-habits!

We have the right goal, but how will we achieve it?

Will we use willpower?

Yeah, right.

Willpower means we have to make a conscious choice, every time. That doesn't work. Depending on willpower is how we failed on our previous goals.

Remember all those New Year's resolutions? Year after year we set those resolutions and fail. Did we feel slightly delusional?

And what is the definition of insanity? Doing the same thing over and over and hoping for a different result.

Okay. Forget willpower. That is not a good plan for us.

Instead? Mini-habits!

What are mini-habits?

Small things that we can do easily, day after day, that eventually become … automatic.

Stephen Guise has an entire book on the science of mini-habits. He explains that if we pick a habit so small that we can do it on our worst day, then we will continue doing that small habit.

Now, we are all familiar with habits. Habits are something we do without thinking. We don't have to make conscious decisions every time we do them. Here are some examples of our habits.

- We brush our teeth every day. Over time, we have good dental hygiene.
- We put on clothes every morning before leaving the house. This happens automatically, every time, without conscious thought. (Well, we hope it does, anyway.)
- We eat with a fork and spoon. We don't have to make that choice every meal.
- We grab a dozen donuts on the way to work. (Okay, not every habit is a good habit.)

Habits happen.

Instead of willpower, we will achieve our goal with habits. But not big habits. Not hard habits. With small, easy-to-do mini-habits.

We will allow the power of habits to move us effortlessly to our goals. Now, how refreshing is that?

Examples of mini-habits for meeting people.

Something small. Something easy.

Something we can do regularly.

We will let our mini-habit put us in front of new people to meet ... automatically.

Ready?

- Say "Hi" to one stranger a day.
- Attend one party every weekend.
- Walk our dog on the lake path every evening.
- Join the weekly hiking club.
- Join a bowling league.
- Send out one message to someone new on social media every day.

Easy? Yes.

Will our encounters with new people accumulate over time? Yes.

Will we reach our goal of meeting new people? Yes.

But, what if we have a different goal?

Then we create a mini-habit that makes achieving that goal ... automatic.

For example, let's imagine that we sell skincare. We want to earn a retailing award from our company. To do this, we calculate that we have to do two skincare parties a month. What kind of mini-habit could we create to make this possible? Here are some examples.

- Send out one hosting invitation a day. We don't care about our daily results. But, over time, we know that some people will accept our invitation to host a party.
- Ask one friend a day to pass on our hosting invitation pack to one of their friends.
- Follow up with one of our current customers every day, and offer them a chance to host a party.
- Give away a hosting invitation pack once a day when out and about.
- Give a free skincare lecture at the community center twice a month. Over time, some of the attendees will want to host a party.

None of these activities are hard. We would pick one or two, and over time, the results would accumulate.

What if we had a goal to overcome our fear of public speaking?

What mini-habit could we create that would ease our fear of public speaking? Here are some examples.

- Every day, do a 30-second mini-speech to one person sitting in a chair.

- Join Toastmasters. The weekly meetings are fun to attend.
- Offer to do a 15-second testimonial at every regular opportunity meeting.
- Say "Hi" to one stranger a day to help us overcome our fear of talking to strangers.
- Offer to introduce speakers at regional meetings.
- Practice our speech in front of a mirror every morning after brushing our teeth.

What if we wanted to get in shape to run a mile?

- Put on our running shoes once a day. Once they are on, it would be easy to walk or run a little bit.
- Park our car farther from the front door at work.
- Start walking our dog. In time we will be jogging a bit with our dog.
- Walk to a different donut shop, farther from our home.
- Buy an elliptical machine. Spend 15 seconds a day on it. Once on the machine, we will tend to use it longer.

Mini-habits are fun.

Why? Because they make it difficult to fail. They are so easy to do that we don't have to make big decisions to take action.

Over time, habits create results.

So instead of depending on erratic willpower, we will use the consistent power of mini-habits to reach our chosen goal.

Want to know more about habits for our network marketing business?

Here is a complete book on habits for network marketers.

The title is *3 Easy Habits For Network Marketing: Automate Your MLM Success.*

NEED MORE HELP WITH GOALS?

In this chapter, we will cover some common tips and tricks for goal-setting. We may have heard these before, but we may not have put them into action. Choose which tips might make goal-setting easier for us.

Think big, start small.

Big goals give us big energy. We need this energy to reach our vision of the future. Having a big goal is nice, but to achieve that goal? We will want to break the big goal into smaller goals. A smaller goal might be 30 days or 90 days.

For example, maybe our big goal is to earn enough in our network marketing business to quit our job. We want time freedom and a chance to express ourselves. It is unlikely that we will achieve that goal in 30 days or in 90 days.

After careful consideration, we feel that our big goal can be achieved in 18 months. So, we break our 18-month goal into six smaller 90-day plans.

When we break our timeline up into smaller segments, such as 90 days, it is easier to stay on track. Our progress (or lack of progress) will be easy to spot. Plus, we don't want our goal to become boring. Every 90 days we will have a fresh goal to keep us excited.

Or, maybe our style of living is more immediate. In that case, we might break up our big goal into monthly, or even weekly goals. We want our goals to feel right for us so that every day is a great day!

Bottom line? It is easier to break up big goals into smaller goals.

The present vs. the future.

Our subconscious mind looks for opportunities and resources to move us ahead in our goals. Here is a little trick to help us train our subconscious mind.

Our subconscious mind understands the present. It does not understand the future very well. When we talk to our subconscious mind, we should use the words, "I am …" We should talk to our subconscious minds in the present tense to get better results.

We shouldn't say to our subconscious mind, "I want to be a Diamond in my business." Instead, we should talk to our subconscious mind by saying, "I am a Diamond in my business." Our subconscious mind will think and act like a Diamond.

Think about it. If we think like a Diamond, and act like a Diamond, what do you think we will become? A Diamond.

Don't panic.

We can modify our goal at any time. This is not a four-year commitment for a university degree. What is important is that we start now. We start our mini-habit and observe our experience. We will know if this goal and mini-habit feels right for us or not.

There is nothing wrong with refining our goal to make it even better for us.

Do three things every day to move closer to the goal.

Consistent action brings consistent results. If we do three things every day that move us toward our goal, what do you think will eventually happen? Yes, we will reach our goal.

These don't have to be big things. They could be as small as talking to three different people that day. Or, following up with three of our previous contacts. It might be attending a seminar or training.

If we do three things every day to move closer to our goals, that adds up to over 1,000 positive actions in one year. That is a lot of momentum and activity pushing us to our goal.

Get ready for action the night before.

When would be a good time to make the list of three things we are going to do to move us toward our goal? The night before. We don't want to wake up in the morning and say to ourselves, "What am I going to do today?"

The best time to make the list of our three actions is the night before. As an added bonus, our subconscious mind can be thinking about these three actions while we sleep.

Using triggers to help us form the mini-habit.

In the beginning, we have to use some willpower to get things done. Later, when it is a habit, it will happen automatically. So how do we develop this habit? With triggers.

In the last example, we made a list of three action things we can do for the next day. We want to make the list the night before.

To assure this will happen, we will set the alarm on our smart phone for 10 PM every evening. When the alarm goes off, we will think, "Have I made my list of three things yet? If not, I need to do it now."

Over time, we won't need that trigger. Our habit will be automatic. We need triggers to remind us early in our habit-formation days.

Start within 24 hours.

Thinking is great, but action makes things happen. We want to take action immediately. Start within the first 24 hours. Don't wait until we have the perfect goal. Remember, we can always adjust the goal as we go.

Action is what counts.

Write down our goal.

Something magical happens when we actually write our goal down. It only takes a few seconds, so let's use that magic.

Since we are writing down our goal, we could have it appear in many different places. On our bathroom mirror, on our refrigerator, inside of our wallet or purse, on the dashboard of our car.

Every time we see this goal, it should bring a smile to our face. If it doesn't bring a smile to our face, we know we chose the wrong goal.

Not motivated?

What if we set our goal and feel no passion or motivation? Maybe we procrastinate?

Hmm. That is a hint.

If we have to motivate ourselves, we should ask, "Do I have the right goal for me?"

If our goal fits our color personality and values, we should look forward to working on our goal automatically. So instead of trying to fix our motivation, maybe we just have the wrong goal.

This often happens when we choose a goal to impress others, to conform to peer pressure, or to make someone else happy.

We put our efforts where our focus is.

We can either focus on our goals, or our problems. If we have no goals, we will only concentrate on our problems. This is another reason to set our own goals now.

If we focus on our goals, we build consistency. Everyone knows that consistency over time means progress. It is just that easy.

THE BIG PAYOFF.

Goals attract followers.

Most people feel lost, and just drift through life. They will eagerly follow us … if we know where we are going, and have a plan to get there. Here is an example.

Picking the right caravan.

Imagine that we are lost in the middle of the Sahara Desert. Not a pleasant experience. It is hot. We are thirsty. We hate the same boring sand dune scenery. A shower, an ice cream sundae, and an airplane ticket home sound perfect. If only we could get to civilization.

A group of nomads approach us. Frantically, we wave to them to stop their caravan. The leader says, "Hey, what are you doing out here alone? That is a pretty stupid thing to be doing."

We answer, "We are lost. Terribly lost. We would love to come with you if we could. By the way, where are you going?"

The nomad leader says, "Going? We are already here. We are nomads. We travel the desert. In fact, I have been roaming the desert since I was born. So, where are we going? I don't know, but we will arrive there tomorrow or next week or next month."

Wow. That isn't what we wanted to hear. We politely say farewell to the leader and wait for the next caravan.

The next day, a new caravan comes along. Again, we run up to the caravan's leader and say, "Where are you going?"

The leader answers, "We are on our way to Casablanca. We will arrive on the 4th. Next, we will take the traders' route to Algiers. We arrive in Algiers on the 22nd and pick up new camels. Then, it is onward to Tunisia for the annual camel rodeo. Would you like to come along?"

Our reply? "You bet!" Finally we can follow someone who knows where he is going. Now we are on our way to civilization, a nice shower, an ice cream sundae and that airplane ride home.

When we want to achieve a goal, or just have a better life, who do we follow? The person who is lost and unfocused? Or, do we prefer following the leader who knows where he is going?

The answer is obvious. And other people feel that way too. They want to follow a focused leader who knows where he or she is going.

And, that focused leader can be us!

We want focused goals. We want to know where we are going and how to get there. Then, the world will crowd around us and ask to join us on our journey. We call this attraction marketing.

The world is full of followers, people desperate for some direction in their lives. These people stand in awe of the few leaders who realize they can choose their own goals and direction. Once we decide where we are going, we will become one of those rare beacons that people flock to.

Yes, it is almost unbelievable that so few people will set their own goals in life. Most of these people are content to observe our goals, and decide to come along for the ride.

Will this have an effect on our network marketing business? Absolutely!

What happens when our natural market of contacts learns that we have a focused goal? They want to ask us for guidance and leadership. All we have to do is let other people know about our goals. When others know that we have a direction in our lives and have a plan ... magic happens. We can expect reactions such as these:

- A co-worker says, "Hey! That is a good idea. I thought we were sentenced to this job for life. I want to come along with you and build a business too!"

- A neighbor says, "Hold on there. If you are going to be earning some part-time extra income, don't leave me out. Let me in on your secret."

- A cousin calls us and says, "I heard you plan to build a full-time business and leave your job. I don't like my job much either. Could you tell me how this works?"

- Our prospect at the business opportunity meeting says, "I like where this opportunity can take me. I want to join you. You are going to the top, and I want to hang onto your coattails."

See the difference our personal goals make in other people's lives? They become eager prospects for our network marketing opportunity.

And what is the lesson here?

Should we keep our goals secret and hidden from the rest of the world? Or should we share our goals and help others who are desperately looking for someone to follow?

Let's help others by sharing our goals with them.

Acronyms for those who love them.

Some of us remember things better when we use acronyms. Here is a complete chapter of some famous goal acronyms to choose from.

SMART.

We read about SMART goals in the management books from the last century. It is a proven system that complements our personality and value goal-setting. If you are a yellow personality, you will like it. If you are a green personality, you will love it. Greens love structured things. Even red personalities love that they can measure their success with SMART goals. Here are what the letters in SMART stand for.

"S" is for Specific.

Be as specific as possible. Why? To make sure we get exactly what we want. If we are vague, we may end up getting what we don't want.

Here is an example. We wish to own a big business, but the business ends up running our lives. We have no time to enjoy our wealth or our family.

Instead, our goal should have been more specific. Maybe our goal would be to have a medium-sized business that ran itself. Then, we would have time to spend our money and be with our family.

The second reason to be specific is that it makes it easier to visualize. Saying that we want a new home is vague and hard to see in our minds.

Instead, we want to know exactly how many stories the house will be, how many bedrooms, how many bathrooms, whether it has a pool or not … and more. We even want to know where our house should be located.

In our network marketing businesses? Our specific goals should be the pin level or rank that we wish to achieve, a specific sales volume, or growth goals for our team.

"M" is for Measurable.

Having a good feeling is hard to measure. So our goals should have accomplishments that we can measure. This will keep our progress consistent. Here are a few things that we could measure:

- How many people do I need to talk to per day?

- How many people do I need to sponsor?

- How many people in my downline should pass a leadership test?

- What do I need to do every day?

"A" is for Achievable.

It is great to think big, but we have to think realistically as well. Can we become the top income earner in under 90 days? Probably not.

Will we earn a full-time income in 30 days? Starting from zero, probably not.

But what can we achieve? Here are some examples:

- A promotion to Assistant Supervisor in the next 30 days.
- Five new customers for our products.
- Two new guests to bring to each weekly opportunity meeting.
- A promotion for our best friend.
- Public speaking classes to be more confident.

"R" is for Relevant.

Make sure our goals are congruent with our personality color and values. Our goals should be what **we** want, not what our sponsor wants. This is our business. If these are our true goals, it will be easy to stay focused.

There are many ways to earn money. We want to avoid distraction by focusing on our network marketing business. If we are trying to earn money by simultaneously balancing four or five income opportunities, we won't have the focus to reach the top in our business.

"T" is for Timely.

Do humans like to procrastinate? Of course. Whenever there is a big project, we put things off until the last moment. Then, we frantically rush to finish our project.

So what would happen if our goals did not have a deadline? We would delay any activity ... forever. That is why our goals must have deadlines.

Can anyone use SMART goals?

What about the yellow and blue personalities? The SMART technique might seem a little dry and regimented.

For those outgoing blue personalities, SMART goals could be a little boring. But not to worry, SMART goals are only one way to keep us focused.

Red personalities like SMART goals because there is accountability and measurement.

Yellow and green personalities do well with SMART goals also. They like the checklist aspect and feel secure that it will keep them on track.

Ready for a test?

Here is a list of goals. Read the list and guess which personality created this list. Ready?

- Pay off the mortgage early.
- Send the kids to college without using a college loan.
- Invest in real estate.

- Save 3% of my paycheck for retirement.
- Give 20% to charity, instead of 10%.
- Plan for our weekly date night.
- Have two years' salary in savings.

What did you guess?

Green? Yellow?

Once we understand the different color personalities, we see why we need goals that match what we want.

It is easier to take ownership of our goals when they match our internal view of the world.

More acronyms?

Here are some of the other acronyms our teams can use to create goals.

WEIRD.

Yes, this is a real acronym for goal-setting. Who could resist such a memorable name? Let's take a look at what it means.

"W" is for Write It Down.

Write it down. Yes, for the reds, it might be very professional on a brand-new sheet of paper with a specific action plan. But for the blues it could be on a Post-It note they found in their junk drawer.

The act of writing helps our brain remember our goals. We want to use every little tip and trick we can to guarantee our success.

Where or how we write our goals is not as important as the writing act itself.

"E" is for Entertaining.

Entertaining? A magic word for the blue personalities. If this goal can be entertaining, it will create internal happiness in every blue personality. This is something they can look forward to every day.

Meet new people? Here's a chance for the blue personalities to talk to people from the moment they wake up in the morning until they fall asleep at night. That would be a typical blue personality goal.

"I" is for Impossible.

This may sound like the wrong word to use with goal-setting, but for some it works. Some people enjoy doing the impossible (or what some people think is impossible.)

Can you guess which personality this would be?

Yes, the red personalities love the recognition of doing the impossible, setting records, and breaking boundaries. Here is their chance to prove the critics wrong. Taking on the impossible can be addictive.

"R" is for Reactions.

Who loves attention? Blue and red personalities. Reaction and recognition from others is a strong motivating force. This is good to have when the going gets difficult. The desire to be noticed helps overcome fear and procrastination. It works for some people. Are you one of them?

"D" is for Dedicated.

Yellow personalities find it easy to dedicate effort to a cause. A goal that is bigger than themselves means they can help others, not just themselves. This sense of responsibility lifts them to higher levels of action.

We know if it is the right goal for us when we wake up in the morning and feel motivated to do our daily actions for our goal.

The big goals are the memorable ones.

Sometimes our goals are so crazy that no one will believe us. So why such big goals? Because no one remembers small goals. The bigger the goals, the bigger the motivation. It is the emotional kick we get from big goals that can help us break through our limitations.

Here are some examples of crazy goals.

Let's go back to the 1950s, when someone had the idea to place a human on the moon. How many people said it was crazy? How many people said it was impossible?

But there were a few people that said, "We can do it. We will figure it out. We will make it happen."

Placing a human on the moon didn't happen until the next decade, but it did happen. How? The people who set that goal worked hard. They had a focused goal. And they believed in the impossible.

Did people around the world watch the moon landing? Yes.

Have there been articles in magazines and newspapers about the moon landing? Yes.

Our big goals can be straight-up crazy, but well worth it in the end.

But like every goal, these believers had to start somewhere. And how did they do it? By starting with smaller goals that got them closer to the big goal. For example, they had to:

- Design and build a new rocket.
- Train astronauts.
- Test unmanned flights.

Here are some other crazy goal examples.

Imagine the 1400s when explorers dreamed about sailing across the Atlantic. How many people thought they were crazy? Tiny wooden ship, dependent upon the wind, with a compass, the sun and the stars to guide them ... these explorers were crazy!

Big, unbelievable goals can become real. The first step is to think … bigger!

Have you ever heard of a bucket list? These are big goals to the person creating the list.

Here are some examples of "bucket list" goals. Some are big goals. Some goals might seem small to us, but huge to the people who put them on their lists.

- Hike to the base camp of Everest.
- Try to stay warm at the ice hotel in Sweden.
- Feed the monkeys in Roatan.
- Go backstage at a concert to meet your favorite performer.
- Write a book.
- Start a blog.
- Ride a horse in Rocky Mountain National Park.
- Become an extra in a sitcom or movie.
- Rent a suite at the Super Bowl.
- Visit all the Hawaiian Islands.
- Drive a monster truck.
- Ride in a hot air balloon at Maasai Mara.
- Captain a sailboat.
- Ski down a black diamond route.
- Eat an iconic food in the city where it originated.
- Run the Boston Marathon.
- Kiss the Blarney Stone.

- Walk the Great Wall.
- Hike down the Grand Canyon.
- Wear lederhosen at Octoberfest in Munich.
- Ride the canals in Venice in a gondola.
- Sit front row at the Stanley Cup finals.
- Become an elephant trainer for a day.
- Visit all the Disney parks.
- Cruise around the world for 90 days.
- Purchase a ticket to space.
- Take a dance class.
- Bungy jump in New Zealand.
- Wear skinny jeans.
- Have a spa day.
- Golf at an invitation-only course.
- Shop on Rodeo Drive.
- Become a high roller in Vegas.
- Fly in a private jet.
- Take a flying lesson.
- Have an all-about-me week.
- Zipline in Costa Rica.
- Learn Spanish.
- Tandem skydive in the Florida Keys.
- Swim with the stingrays.

One more acronym?

Sure, why not? We saved the fun acronym for last. Blue personalities love this acronym the best.

STUPID.

Do you feel unique? A bit contrarian? Tired of your SMART-goal friends?

Do you cringe when people say something is impossible?

Do people question your sanity?

Do people describe you as unique?

Then this might be the goal-setting acronym for you.

"S" is for Specific.

Like we mentioned earlier in this chapter, if we are not specific, we may feel unhappy when we reach our goals. The more description and detail we can add to our goals, the better.

"T" is for Tiny.

Yes, tiny. Why? So we can celebrate each tiny goal we accomplish on the way to our big goal.

We can create a habit of accomplishing, celebrating, and achieving. And who likes to celebrate the most? The blue personalities, of course.

So instead of one huge goal, think tiny, multiple goals.

"U" is for Unrealistic.

The crazier our goals, the better. Some people get addicted to crazy, and this addiction gives them the fuel to push on against tough odds.

Several tiny goals create huge goals that stretch our attitude and belief. Dreaming big helps us grow as individuals. There is a certain element of mystery in big goals. This keeps life interesting.

"P" is for Party.

Why limit the celebration to when we reach goals? Why not make the goals themselves fun?

If our goal activities are fun to do, then we will party every day while working toward our goals.

For example, if we love travel, and our goal is to talk to five new people a day, what could we do to make this more fun? Well, we could go to the local travel agents' convention and talk to five travel agents. They would be fun to talk to!

Sure, this is easy for the blue personalities. They can have fun anywhere, anytime. But what about the red personalities? Can they have fun?

Yes! The red personalities will create a goal that requires daily accountability and reporting. They look forward to breaking each day's records and reporting their accomplishments to their accountability partners.

"I" is for Impossible.

Rebels, non-conformists, and one-of-a-kind individuals thrive on the impossible. Why? Maybe it is the satisfaction of proving others wrong.

Carrying the badge of "overcoming the impossible" brings meaning to today's goal-achieving activities.

What better adventure can there be than challenging the impossible?

"D" is for Dedicated.

Making a difference. This is one of the higher values for us as humans. We want to leave a legacy. It is easier to dedicate our efforts to a big financial goal, or to a big humanitarian goal, than to a tiny goal. Few people get excited about reaching a goal of $50 in commissions. But a goal to put an orphan through school is something we can dedicate our efforts to.

In conclusion.

Goals work … if we choose the right goals for us.

Why work on goals that someone else gives us when we can work on the perfect goals for our lives?

When our goals are right for us, motivation is automatic. No more stress, procrastination, or worry.

Instead, every day will be a fun day. Working on our goals will be enjoyable, not a chore.

Have fun on the journey to your goals.

THANK YOU.

Thank you for purchasing and reading this book. I hope you found some ideas that will work for you.

Before you go, would it be okay if I asked a small favor? Would you take just one minute and leave a sentence or two reviewing this book online? Your review can help others choose what they will read next. It would be greatly appreciated by many fellow readers.

I travel the world 240+ days each year.
Let me know if you want me to stop in your
area and conduct a live Big Al training.

→ **BigAlSeminars.com** ←

FREE Big Al Training Audios

Magic Words for Prospecting

plus Free eBook and the Big Al Report!

→ **BigAlBooks.com/free** ←

More Big Al Books

Closing for Network Marketing
Getting Prospects Across The Finish Line

Here are 46 years' worth of our best closes. All of these closes are kind and comfortable for prospects, and rejection-free for us.

Pre-Closing for Network Marketing
"Yes" Decisions Before The Presentation

Instead of selling to customers with facts, features and benefits, let's talk to prospects in a way they like. We can now get that "yes" decision first, so the rest of our presentation will be easy.

The One-Minute Presentation
Explain Your Network Marketing Business Like A Pro

Learn to make your business grow with this efficient, focused business presentation technique.

Retail Sales for Network Marketers
How to Get New Customers for Your MLM Business

Learn how to position your retail sales so people are happy to buy. Don't know where to find customers for your products and services? Learn how to market to people who want what you offer.

Getting "Yes" Decisions
What insurance agents and financial advisors can say to clients

In the new world of instant decisions, we need to master the words and phrases to successfully move our potential clients to lifelong clients. Easy … when we can read their minds and service their needs immediately.

3 Easy Habits For Network Marketing
Automate Your MLM Success

Use these habits to create a powerful stream of activity in your network marketing business.

Motivation. Action. Results.
How Network Marketing Leaders Move Their Teams

Learn the motivational values and triggers our team members have, and learn to use them wisely. By balancing internal motivation and external motivation methods, we can be more effective motivators.

The Four Color Personalities for MLM
The Secret Language for Network Marketing

Learn the skill to quickly recognize the four personalities and how to use magic words to translate your message.

Ice Breakers!
How To Get Any Prospect To Beg You For A Presentation

Create unlimited Ice Breakers on-demand. Your distributors will no longer be afraid of prospecting, instead, they will love prospecting.

How To Get Instant Trust, Belief, Influence and Rapport!
13 Ways To Create Open Minds By Talking To The Subconscious Mind

Learn how the pros get instant rapport and cooperation with even the coldest prospects. The #1 skill every new distributor needs.

First Sentences for Network Marketing
How To Quickly Get Prospects On Your Side

Attract more prospects and give more presentations with great first sentences that work.

How to Follow Up With Your Network Marketing Prospects
Turn Not Now Into Right Now!

Use the techniques in this book to move your prospects forward from "Not Now" to "Right Now!"

How To Prospect, Sell And Build Your Network Marketing Business With Stories

If you want to communicate effectively, add your stories to deliver your message.

26 Instant Marketing Ideas To Build Your Network Marketing Business

176 pages of amazing marketing lessons and case studies to get more prospects for your business immediately.

How To Build Network Marketing Leaders
Volume One: Step-By-Step Creation Of MLM Professionals

This book will give you the step-by-step activities to actually create leaders.

How To Build Network Marketing Leaders
Volume Two: Activities And Lessons For MLM Leaders

You will find many ways to change people's viewpoints, to change their beliefs, and to reprogram their actions.

51 Ways and Places to Sponsor New Distributors
Discover Hot Prospects For Your Network Marketing Business

Learn the best places to find motivated people to build your team and your customer base.

Big Al's MLM Sponsoring Magic

How To Build A Network Marketing Team Quickly

This book shows the beginner exactly what to do, exactly what to say, and does it through the eyes of a brand-new distributor.

Public Speaking Magic

Success and Confidence in the First 20 Seconds

By using any of the three major openings in this book, we can confidently start our speeches and presentations without fear.

Worthless Sponsor Jokes

Network Marketing Humor

Here is a collection of worthless sponsor jokes from 25 years of the "Big Al Report." Network marketing can be enjoyable, and we can have fun making jokes along the way.

Start SuperNetworking!

5 Simple Steps to Creating Your Own Personal Networking Group

Start your own personal networking group and have new, pre-sold customers and prospects come to you.

How To Get Kids To Say Yes!

Using the Secret Four Color Languages to Get Kids to Listen

Turn discipline and frustration into instant cooperation. Kids love to say "yes" when they hear their own color-coded language.

BIGALBOOKS.COM

ABOUT THE AUTHORS

Keith Schreiter has 20+ years of experience in network marketing and MLM. He shows network marketers how to use simple systems to build a stable and growing business.

So, do you need more prospects? Do you need your prospects to commit instead of stalling? Want to know how to engage and keep your group active? If these are the types of skills you would like to master, you will enjoy his "how-to" style.

Keith speaks and trains in the U.S., Canada, and Europe.

Tom "Big Al" Schreiter has 40+ years of experience in network marketing and MLM. As the author of the original "Big Al" training books in the late '70s, he has continued to speak in over 80 countries on using the exact words and phrases to get prospects to open up their minds and say "YES."

His passion is marketing ideas, marketing campaigns, and how to speak to the subconscious mind in simplified, practical ways. He is always looking for case studies of incredible marketing campaigns that give usable lessons.

As the author of numerous audio trainings, Tom is a favorite speaker at company conventions and regional events.